Not the Place to Ignore Me

Lessons in Faith from a Deadly Ambush

Joshua Motes

in cooperation with

Not the Place to Ignore Me: Lessons in Faith from a Deadly Ambush
Joshua Motes

AbandONEd Communications
Colorado Springs, Colorado
Library of Congress Control Number: 2013902343
In cooperation with MULTIPLi Communications

DEDICATION

This book is dedicated to my Lord and Savior, Jesus, and to the soldiers and noncommissioned officers of the Military Police Platoon, 2nd Special Troops Battalion. It was the honor and privilege of a lifetime to serve beside you as your platoon leader in Afghanistan.

"Jesters"

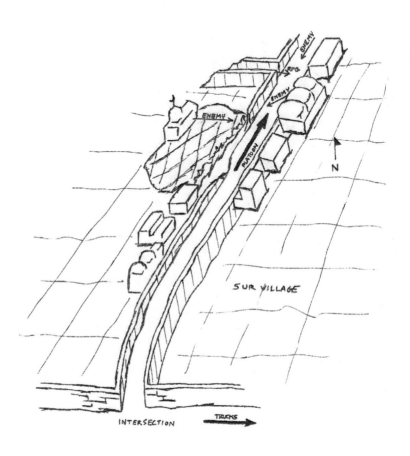

Sur Village, area of interest.

TABLE OF CONTENTS

FOREWORD

It has been five years since I first encountered Joshua Motes. It was at a Sunday night gathering designed for college students, called "the Link." I was the directional leader for the Link and Joshua was a college student at the University of Arkansas. He had already served one military tour in Iraq as a young 19-year-old man, and come out alive. Although his life was spared from an improvised explosive device, his heart was hard and his ears were closed.

I remember the night we met very well. He walked through the student center doors, didn't say a word, sat down by himself, and pretty much crossed his arms through the entire message. For the sake of many, including Joshua, God did not cross His arms that night. Our loving Father had this young man in His cross sights. The journey Joshua has taken since that evening is nothing short of God's miraculous hand in fast action.

Truly, God is raising up a generation much like Saul of Tarsus (Paul)—unashamed trophies of His kindness. Like Paul, Joshua has been blinded, led into Arabia and back out again with a fresh perspective and newfound power. He has discovered the true knowledge of God and his story is one you will never forget.

From the day Joshua started writing *Not the Place to Ignore Me*, I knew its message was an urgent one for the Bride of Christ. The true story of 14 July 2011, is a parable for each of our lives. Whether in Afghanistan, America, or anywhere

1

in between, the principles gleaned from Joshua's experience will offer you a mirror in which to view your own story. It will cause you to look closely at your relationships and re-evaluate your position as a brother, sister, mother, father, husband, or wife. The book you are holding reaches beyond surface talk and broaches a subject we have often forgotten in the American church; spiritual warfare.

Have you wondered why you feel oppressed? Have you thought, as Joshua did that fateful day as he walked into the deserted Afghan cityscape, that something was not right with the picture you were seeing? We sense spiritual realities intuitively, but unless we have a deep understanding of our adversary and his tactics, we will not be able to make sense of our current situation. We may even find ourselves under intense enemy fire.

With great pleasure and passion, I commend to you the book you now hold. It is time for Jesus' bride to pay attention. He alone has the ability to guide us faithfully through the fire and fury of our enemy. His eyes are flames of fire, His hair is white as snow, and there is a sword coming from His mouth. He promised His protection and promotion. He will be faithful to fulfill His promises, if only we will not ignore Him. Truly, this is not the time or place to ignore Him.

Josh Foliart
Founder of MULTIPLi
Author of *Rooted: Reach Deep. Burn Bright. Stand Strong.*
Fayetteville, Arkansas
Fall, 2012

INTRODUCTION

When I returned from Afghanistan in June, 2012, I wondered what it all meant. From the moment I learned I would be deploying to Afghanistan—while attending the Basic Officer Leadership course at Fort Leonard Wood, Missouri—I knew it was from God. My class numbered nearly sixty new lieutenants, but I was the only one deploying following graduation. It confirmed to me the calling God had distinctly placed on my heart back in college.

At the time, I wasn't sure what I wanted to do after college, but once I found Christ, it was clear to me that He wanted me to finish ROTC and commission as an officer. Having lived the enlisted life as an active duty soldier before college, I knew that I would have an influence for Jesus among the men I would inevitably lead.

In June 2012, after a long year of deployment in Afghanistan in support of Operation Enduring Freedom, my platoon and I arrived back at Fort Carson, Colorado. The long road of reintegration was beginning, and I wondered what the past year had been about—what it meant. As time went on, I knew I would receive revelation about my year spent there, but in those first confusing days home, it was still all a mystery.

I had the opportunity to share the story with several close, trusted friends. They all told me I needed to write about it, so this book came to be. God has been faithful, revealing to me what my time in Afghanistan meant. This story is part of that revelation. It is my transparent, humble gift to you, a testament to His love and faithfulness.

This book was written with two intentions. The first is, to provide you with a picture of what it is like to deploy oversees and serve as a soldier in Afghanistan. The United States has been at war for the past decade, and the vast majority of Americans are largely unaware of all that entails. We hear reports of events through television and other media outlets, but they present only tiny glimpses of the picture that do not come close to conveying the daily grind of a deployment or depth of emotion associated with it. Just one half of one percent of Americans serve in the military, and only a fraction of them have actually experienced direct fire combat. As you turn the pages of this book, you will find yourself in the middle of a very exclusive life.

Second, and more importantly, the book was written to empower you with practical lessons for living as a Christian in a world where you fight a very real enemy. Told through a dire series of events in a horrific ambush in Afghanistan, you will find yourself on patrol in a hostile village—a parallel to the life you live in Christ Jesus, today. You will come to discover how oblivious I was to an inevitable and grave danger during an unrepentant, spiritually dry season. You will also discover (or be affirmed in) the sovereignty of God, His incomprehensible grace, and goodness.

Chapter 1

DEPLOYING

"I'm a man under orders; I also give orders. I tell one soldier, 'Go,' and he goes."

Luke 7:8 (MSG)

I wonder what swirling emotions Peter felt when he released the net from his calloused hands, allowing it to fall to the ground. In the net was his livelihood—life as he had always known it for all those years—falling to the ground in a woven array of fibers that had been the rope. For Peter, it must have symbolized the sudden cessation of his relatively comfortable life as a fisherman in the beautiful waters of the Sea of Galilee.

Just yards in front of him stood a quite ordinary looking man, not physically impressive or attractive, yet He had inexplicably captivated Peter with His request: "Come, follow me." In spite of the uncertainty he must have felt, stepping off that boat and out into the unknown, Peter must have looked forward to walking beside this man into inevitable history.

I've been there. Certainly not in the same sense Simon Peter was, standing face to face with Jesus physically, on the shores of the Sea of Galilee. But I too have experienced the emotions, anxieties, and fears of releasing every comfort—everything I knew and loved.

On June 11, 2011, a cool southern Colorado evening, as I walked across the tarmac, I turned my head back towards Pike's Peak just in time to watch the sun disappear behind its dominant face. I remember being struck by how God had established this impressive, fourteen thousand foot mountain as the focal point over Colorado Springs.

As I turned my eyes forward, they locked onto the massive commercial airliner that was about to carry me nearly twenty hours away to one of the greatest unknown, most uncertain times of my life. My rifle was slung across my chest, my sidearm strapped to my leg, and I had an assault bag filled with a few items that would make the journey a little less depressing. As I walked, I couldn't help but wonder if my boots would be walking back towards Pike's Peak a year from now, when we were scheduled to return from our twelve month combat tour in Afghanistan. For now, I was walking away (eventually flying away). But just as Peter no doubt experienced, uncontrolled emotions swirled within me as I contemplated what the coming weeks and months might hold for me, and for my life.

Deployment, as you can probably imagine, is difficult for a soldier. To be honest, when you finally take your seat on the airplane that is going to carry you "over there" (wherever "there" is), it is actually kind of a relief. By that point, you've spent six months doing nothing but train, train, pack your containers, train, pack your personal gear, and train some more. You've spent many days and nights in the "field" (training areas on an Army post), and a rotation to another Army post to "simulate" deployment and combat. You do this under the constant feeling that, inevitably, you will be leaving soon.

In the final few days, particularly the precious hours preceding your "report time," bizarrely, you find yourself thinking, "I am ready to just go." Of course, this is not because you are actually excited to go (though I will confess, there is a little of that), but largely because you just want to get there and get it over with. For the past six months, you have been living with one foot in the door and one outside it.

I am not married, nor do I have children. I cannot imagine what living with one's family is like before leaving. Even as close as I was emotionally to the men under my command, I cannot imagine it. Honestly, it was not talked about. I assume this is because those married soldiers would just rather not discuss it.

Before we made that fateful trek across the tarmac to the uninviting airliner that resembled a coffin more than a Boeing, I watched as soldiers struggled to say goodbye to their wives and children. The wives' wails and tears raged like a Category 5 hurricane. It was in this moment, for the first time in the year or two leading up to deployment, that I was actually thankful I wasn't married.

I could not (and still cannot) understand how these guys leave their families with the full realization that they may never see them again. And the last memory ingrained in their minds is not joyful; it is a dramatic and sorrowful goodbye at a rapid deployment center.

We settled into our seats. Our families and life as we knew it would soon be specks on the earth from ten thousand feet. As we ascended into the Colorado sky and turned East toward uncertainty, I began to think to myself how incredibly thankful I was that I was saved. That in the center of my chest, beneath the uniform, pulsating to the tempo of my heart—Jesus Christ was there. As the airliner climbed into the night sky, I reflected upon the previous few months. I reflected on my salvation. It was so clear that from the point of my submission and acceptance of Jesus, God had funneled me to this point.

I had been well-prepared. I had been here before, deployed to war. Iraq, 2003...I was there. Of course, back then I was a 19-year-old private, responsible only for my weapon and canteen. And though I was responsible for thirty-eight lives now, I had still been here. As I looked out from my aisle seat and saw worry shroud the faces of my 19-year-old privates, I could empathize. When I sat in their seat nearly ten years earlier, like many of them, I was unsaved. Back then, I had been totally clueless to the grave danger of my eternal life, in any capacity, let alone a war.

At my center, I knew that I was not deploying to fight a war, support an agenda, or develop a country. I was deploying for the hearts of the soldiers God had entrusted to my command. I was deploying to use Afghanistan as a catalyst to be truly intentional in their lives for the Gospel of Jesus Christ.

At my center, I knew that I was not deploying to fight a war, support an agenda, or develop a country. I was deploying for the hearts of the soldiers God had entrusted to my command. I was deploying to use Afghanistan as a catalyst to be truly intentional in their lives for the Gospel of Jesus Christ.

Just as in the preceding months, as I relaxed back into my "lowest-bidder produced" seat, I thought to myself: *Thank you, Jesus, that this time, this deployment, I will endure through your strength, not my own. And Lord, if I lose my life in the place this plane will land in another twenty hours, I am certain of where I will be—unlike the last time. Thank you, Jesus.*

As we reached our cruising altitude and the cabin lights were dimmed, I donned my headphones, expecting to drift into unconscious oblivion. Prior to fading away, I thought back to the previous night. All my personal belongings were collected in storage, my life consolidated between a duffel bag and rucksack. The verse God placed upon me the previous night came roaring back into focus: "Consecrate yourselves, for tomorrow the Lord will do amazing things among you" (Joshua 3:5). *consecrate* means *to set one's self apart.* My affairs were in order. My phone was disconnected. I had no connection to the life I knew and was comfortable in; other than a collection of family members and a storage unit. I was covered in prayer. The Word was on my tongue.

I was ready to commit all my focus and energy to accomplishing both the Lord's and United States Army's mission. Little did I know, a little more than a month removed from the comfort of my commercial airline seat, I would find myself in the physical and spiritual fight of my life.

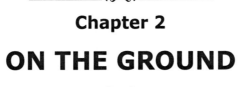

Chapter 2

ON THE GROUND

"I have become an alien in a foreign land."

Exodus 2:22

We had been airborne for over an hour. This flight was nowhere near as comfortable or accommodating as the commercial airliner we had the privilege of flying on from Colorado Springs to Manas, Kyrgyzstan. The C-17 Globemaster III, a large, very intimidating United States Air Force cargo plane, with a nose that, when viewed directly from the front, looked like a menacing bull running down an unfortunate soul on the streets of Spain. As intimidating and uncomfortable as this plane was, I was quite familiar with them. Growing up in Long Beach, California, my home and schools were minutes from the Long Beach Airport, "The Home of the USAF C-17" adorned the massive manufacturing hangars located there.

I remember the much needed recesses during elementary school. I would run around or swing from the monkey bars, expending energy—to my teacher's delight—only to hear the roar of the four Pratt & Whitney turbine engines rising from the horizon. I would stop in place, and look up to see the massive "bull" climb into the beautiful Southern California sky over my school for a test flight. The plane I now found myself flying on to Afghanistan had held a special place in my heart from my youth. Everything the plane was that had appealed to my nature as a young boy—big, strong, and powerful—still appealed to me as a 28-year-old man.

As much affinity as I felt with the C-17, I still felt incredibly uncomfortable. The Air Force, in order to transport Army soldiers, graciously fixes rows of seats to the center of the C-17's cargo hull. These seats were apparently designed for individuals under six feet tall. Unfortunately, I found myself in one of them, my legs congested into the seat back in front of me. I had tried to find a seat against the fuselage of the aircraft, to no avail. These seats run the length of the cargo hull on the port and starboard side walls, and are highly sought after because they allow you to extend your legs out into the center.

At this point, because we were no longer flying the "friendly" skies and would be landing in Afghanistan, we were required to be in full gear, including our IOTV (Improved Outer Tactical Vest)—an already uncomfortable contraption—our body armor, and all its associated gear. This meant our seats, already cramped, now had to accommodate our oversized torsos. In addition to being 6'2" and jammed into my seat like a peanut M&M in a thimble, let's just say...I was miserable. So when I heard power reduced from the four turbines, and the crew chief's voice came over the intercom to announce we would be landing soon, I was more than relieved.

Touchdown

Aside from announcing that we would be landing soon, the crew chief also informed us that we would be landing on an unimproved dirt runway. The C-17 was designed with the capability to land on remote, unimproved runways, but I hoped the engineers had actually tested this, as opposed to stating it in a quasi used car salesman pitch to the Air Force in order to get them to purchase the plane.

Landing in a combat zone is always exciting...and dangerous. Such was the case when we descended into Baghdad International Airport in September, 2003. Due to the threat of antiaircraft fire, pilots do not approach the runway in a long, gradual descent as they would if they were making an approach to LAX (where the greatest "enemy" threat is a pigeon flying into an engine). Oh no, they would do a steep, nearly 45-degree drop a short distance from the runway, very hard over level, at the last minute before touchdown.

Now, as we pitched steeply down, I felt like Neil Armstrong and Buzz Aldrin probably felt, descending to the lunar surface, wondering if they were going to add another black crater to the terrain. We held on as the plane jolted and lurched violently, the fuselage straining to handle the turbulent g-forces, as (I imagine) the pilots fought the stick to bring it out. My stomach shot through the roof of the hull as the plane leveled after the sharp descent and we hit the dirt runway of FOB (Forward Operating Base) Farah like a brick falling from a mason's hands from the top a skyscraper. The plane skipped and fought to find grip, as a deafening roar indicated the pilots had applied the brakes and reverse flaps to the strained airframe. The plane grumbled to a halt and daylight pierced the hull. As the cargo ramp was dropped, heat immediately filled the C-17. The feeling that had clung to me for months, the inevitability of "being there," suddenly became my reality in a gust of blinding sun and melting heat. After the ramp was completely down and the engines had been idled, we shuffled out of the plane under the weight of all our gear.

As I stepped off the ramp onto the dusty runway, I looked out over the surrounding terrain. FOB Farah sits in the western expanse of Afghanistan between two mountain ranges, one to the South and one to the North. It is approximately ninety miles East of the Iran/ Afghan border. I was struck by the terrain. It looked like every picture I had ever seen of Mars—a combination of shades of red painted over jagged, intimidating mountains that rose from arid, barren fields.

As we walked from the plane and down the dusty runway to the actual FOB, in an effort to bring a little comfort and sense of "home" to the depressing, unfamiliar environment, I gazed up at the mountain to the North and thought for sure it looked just like a Razorback, the mascot of my alma mater, the University of Arkansas. (In fact, that mountain became known to all my guys as "Razorback Mountain.")

We walked for what seemed like an eternity to our battalion's "footprint" on the FOB. There, we were issued our living quarters and ammunition. In light of all the preparation, all the talk about "being there," and the days of travel, one thing was now abundantly clear...we were on the ground.

Relief in Place

Despite jet lag and the mental and emotional exhaustion of several days of travel, upon arrival at Farah, there was no time to rest. Much work needed to be done before my platoon could begin conducting operations in our area of responsibility.

I immediately sought out my commander, Captain Roy. He had arrived at Farah the week prior to my chalk's arrival. (A "chalk" is simply a group of soldiers.) Captain Roy was a former enlisted soldier who had switched over to the officer side, like me. He was an experienced man. And in 2004, as a lieutenant, he had led his platoon in a highly contested district of Mosul, Iraq. Now a captain, and my company commander, he would establish the patrol schedule that my platoon would execute.

During my initial huddle with Captain Roy, I was introduced to my counterpart, the outgoing platoon leader for the platoon mine would replace. In a deployed environment, this process is called the RIP (Relief in Place). During this time, usually a week, the relieving unit signs for all the departing unit's equipment, conducts left seat/right seat rides (missions to acquaint the arriving unit with the area of operations), and gains as much useful, helpful information as possible from the departing unit.

Over the course of the first few days, I signed for over $14 million worth of TPE (Theater Provided Equipment; equipment specifically designed and deployed for use in Afghanistan), and shadowed my outgoing counterpart. It was the middle of June, which meant two things in Afghanistan: it is extremely hot, and it is the fighting season.

Unlike the United States, where temperature deter-
mines seasons, in Afghanistan, the temperature deter-
mines fighting. The spring, summer, and early fall are all
part of the fighting season, because the weather permits
the Taliban freedom of movement and favorable conditions
to fight under. In the winter, the precipitation causes the
terrain to be unfavorable for their style of combat operations, and their "man jammies" (the pajama suit attire they
sport) do little to protect them from the cold. I found this
skewed view of seasons comical. For us, the Christmas season in Afghanistan was not just a time to rejoice in Jesus'
birth, but also to rejoice that the Taliban were cold and,
therefore, wouldn't fight.

We were in the middle of both the RIP process and
fighting season. The platoon we were replacing still had
responsibilities "outside the wire" (outside the confines
of the FOB, in enemy territory). Until we officially conducted our TOA (Transfer of Authority), the platoon we
were replacing still had a mission to conduct. During
several of our RIP tasks, we had to pause so the outgoing platoon could respond to hostilities within Farah
province.

My third day in country, during our RIP process, I joined
their platoon on one such mission. As I harnessed into my
seat, I felt the same feeling of physical vulnerability I had
felt the first time I went on mission in Iraq, in 2003—a feeling I had long since forgotten. As we rolled outside the wire,
despite my anxiety, I didn't fear the end of my physical life
as I had during my combat tour in Iraq, due to uncertainty
of my eternal life.

Farah, Afghanistan

Our TOA was completed on June 21, 2011. On that day, my platoon assumed all responsibility for the overall security of Farah city and the surrounding area. This was the largest area of operations belonging to our task force, and my platoon was responsible for it. (No pressure!)

If there is a beacon of hope for what Afghanistan could be, it is Farah city. It isn't a huge city, with a population of roughly 30,000, but it is a city nonetheless, and the economic and cultural hub of Western Afghanistan.

In Farah, education is flourishing. In fact, to this day, some of my fondest memories are of driving through the city on patrol and seeing scores of girls walking to class, carrying their textbooks and backpacks. In this country, just a decade before, women were persecuted for not wearing veils and for even attempting to attend schools. This was incredible progress.

There also appeared to be a booming third world version of Wall Street commerce conducted daily in Farah—without violence. Produce and flatbread vendors lined the main street running through the city. Tailor shops produced custom man jammies. (I even had one tailored for me when we stopped in to visit one of the shop owners during a presence patrol.) The local butcher had "fresh-ish" lamb hanging from hooks under the corrugated steel rolled up in front of his shop. The local Afghani "Home Depot" was closely rivaled by Fazl's (the equivalent of Lowe's).

My platoon and I were responsible for all the Farah substations of the Afghan National Police (ANP). Fortunately, they were all led by competent, motivated commanders. I use to love visiting them throughout the week, being able to take my helmet off in their offices, drinking fresh chai tea, and talking about the old days, when they fought the Russians.

Even under the Taliban, Farah benefitted from its geographical location. Because it was so far West, the Taliban's reign never reached its full potential in the city. Don't misunderstand me; I did hear several accounts of Taliban brutality within Farah, however, nothing as significant as what was witnessed to the East, in Kabul, or South, in Kandahar. The people of Farah were beginning to fully realize freedom. Women had come out from beneath the veil. Cell phone use and television viewing were accepted. The overall security of Farah was an example for the rest of the country to follow. I wish the same could be said for the outlying villages. As peaceful as Farah seemed, that peace would instantly disappear for us in less than a month during a visit to one such neighboring village.

᷿᷿
Chapter 3

RECEIVE THE MISSION
᷿᷿

"This was my situation: The heat consumed me in the daytime and the cold at night, and sleep fled from my eyes."

Genesis 31:40

TOA was complete. Our outgoing counterparts had left Farah, on their way back to the United States. For the next year, we could look forward to dirt, heat, sweat, and time. It was late June, and our platoon was preparing to conduct its first mission. My commander, Captain Roy, would publish our patrol schedule with a task and purpose. In the Army, a clear task and purpose are assigned to every mission, and look something like this:

24 June

T (Task): Conduct Mounted Patrol to Sorabad Village,

P (Purpose): IOT (in order to) conduct initial KLE (Key Leader Engagement) with the Shurah leader (a Shurah leader is a tribal or village leader in Afghanistan).

Autonomous

With the patrol schedule published, I would take the tasks and produce a CONOP (Concept of the Operation) for the given mission. This is a two-sheet synopsis of the mission to be conducted. The CONOP for each patrol provides Battalion with vital information—exactly what each patrol will be doing. Think of who, what, when, where, and why. In addition, it also includes a communication plan, a CASE-VAC/MEDEVAC plan (Casualty Evacuation/ Medical Evacuation), actions on contact (basically your what if's should you encounter the enemy), a map or some imagery of where you are going, and a trip ticket (a by truck roster of who is going on the mission).

The trip ticket includes each soldier's battle roster number. This is comprised of each soldier's initials and the last four digits of their social security number. For instance, mine was "JM9855." It also included each soldier's blood type and weapon serial number. A CONOP is essentially your "ticket to ride." Without one, your element (Army term for personnel and equipment allocated to a mission) was going nowhere.

There was generally a short deadline to produce a CONOP for your mission. They had to be submitted for ultimate approval forty-eight to seventy-two hours in advance of the mission. As tedious as developing a CONOP was, I valued it, because it caused me to sit down and methodically think through each phase of the operation and plan for contingencies. However, I must attest, during the last few months of the deployment, I had done them so many times, everything was fairly automatic. Producing a CONOP would take me five minutes, literally.

Generally, the platoon would start preparing the trucks an hour and a half prior to our departure, though that could vary depending on the mission. The guys lived in rudimentary buildings right behind where our row of vehicles were parked, and they learned our vehicles inside and out. When I would arrive for the mission brief, every truck was prepared and running. Radio checks had been conducted to ensure we had communication, fluids had been checked, the weapons were mounted, and the BFT (Blue Force Tracker, a computer based system that links friendly forces across the battlefield) was up and operating. The drivers, taking full ownership of these steads, would even wipe the thick armored glass clean of the dust and grime that inevitably accumulated due to the Martian atmosphere. Pre-mission preparation was convenient for the "Joes" (slang for junior enlisted soldiers) because of the proximity of the vehicles to their living quarters. This was especially true when we would have a QRF (Quick Reaction Force) mission at 2 or 3 a.m.

About thirty minutes out from our SP (start point) time, we would conduct the mission brief. My senior squad leader, Staff Sergeant Joseph Parks, or I, would brief the soldiers on the mission and contingency plans. During the mission brief, the soldiers get a detailed overview of the mission we would be conducting. This includes the mission statement, which would go something like this: "Jester 1 conducts a mounted patrol to the village of Sorabad in order to conduct an initial KLE with the Sorabad Shurah leader in an effort to gain demographics, position towards coalition forces, and address security concerns." Once the mission statement has been pitched, the specifics follow, including the route of travel, travel speed, communication, MEDEVAC plan, and actions on contact.

I have always been incredibly impressed by the profes-
sionalism of these soldiers, young men in their early twen-
ties. Though few had education beyond high school, I was
always amazed at their copious note-taking and diligence
in asking the right questions. I believe these young soldiers
conducting combat operations in Afghanistan know better
than just about anyone the dire need to pay attention to
detail and follow instructions. I often thought to myself,
with only a year (and some change) removed from a college classroom: *How much greater would college students
do academically if they understood the need for detail that
my soldiers of the same age did?*

At the conclusion of the mission brief, we would
conduct a few rehearsals, essentially acting out our
battle drills, for example, what to do in the event of an
IED (Improvised Explosive Device) strike, or a vehicle
recovery. For more complex missions, for example, if we
would be doing a dismounted movement, the drills would
include maneuvering on the enemy or breaking contact.
With the pre-mission necessities complete, we would
load up in the trucks. A part of the truck commander's
responsibility is to ensure that each soldier is harnessed
into the seat and the doors are battle locked. Once those
final checks are complete, I would receive the report over
the radio that our element was "Red Condition 1," meaning, we were good to roll.

Leaving the Wire

On the very first mission out of FOB Farah, I sat in my seat
in the second vehicle in the convoy as we maneuvered
through the serpentine gate and ventured outside the wire.

The reality of the responsibility I carried weighed heavily on me. I was ultimately responsible for over twenty human lives, nearly $14 million worth of Army property, and everything we did or failed to do. I was sweating. No matter how educated, experienced, or prepared I may have felt prior to that moment, as the massive Michelin tires of my MAT-V (Mine Resistant, Ambush Protected All-Terrain Vehicle) turned out of the confines of the FOB, I realized just how unprepared I was. Apart from the Holy Spirit and God's sovereignty, I was grossly unqualified for such an undertaking.

Shewan

The week that began on July 3, 2011 is one I will never forget. We had been conducting autonomous operations for two weeks. But on July 3rd, we were patrolling the East district of Farah city on foot with the ANP of Substation 4 (the police responsible for this district). It was hot—I mean brutally hot. We were about two miles into our patrol when I got a call on the radio from Staff Sergeant Parks, who was back at our trucks with a small contingent of the platoon.

"Jester 6, this is Jester 1—over."

"Go for Jester 6," I responded.

"Bandit Company is in contact in Shewan right now, we are instructed to get up there immediately—over," Staff Sergeant Parks advised me.

I acknowledged, "Roger, we'll move back to the trucks now, continue to monitor the situation, and update me as necessary, Jester 6—out."

Bandit (our sister company in the task force) was engaged in fierce fighting in Shewan, a village just outside of their outpost. Shewan was a highly contested Taliban hotbed, and a major center of opium and marijuana cultivation—a key source of revenue for the Taliban.

Bandit had been conducting a routine dismounted patrol in the village, and had come under intense fire. Battalion was informing our platoon that we needed to respond immediately. Parks informed me that our presence was requested, like yesterday, emphasizing the severity of the situation. I turned to Captain Mohammad Evaz, the Substation 4 commander (who, coincidentally, looked like an Afghani version of Wyatt Earp), and said, "We have to go." I informed my dismounted element, and we double-timed it back to the trucks.

That afternoon, our element had established observation points on the highway outside of Shewan, and we essentially remained there for the next week. Battalion knew there was a serious Taliban presence in the village, and that it would have to be dealt with. In the week following Bandit's TIC (Troops in Contact) with the Taliban, my platoon was OPCONed (Operationally Controlled) by Bandit. For the next week, we did not return to Farah.

While with Bandit at their base, Shewan Garrison, Battalion was devising a plan to essentially start from the South and move North, systematically clearing the village. All the while, we were living out of small packs in a tiny tent. It was a total transient life, and we knew we were ultimately there to bolster Bandit's numbers. Each night leading up to the incursion, we sat out on the highway separating the garrison from the village, watching and listening for Taliban activity.

On Sunday, July 10th, the operation commenced. Bandit moved in first with minimal trouble. They made it all the way to the dry riverbed on the North side of the village, approximately a two kilometer movement through densely congested mud huts and rod iron gate arrangements. Around 1300 (1 p.m.) we initiated our movement.

It was early afternoon in the middle of July in Afghanistan, and it was already 140 degrees. Each one of us was carrying in excess of 80 pounds of ammunition, water, and an assortment of other mission essential items. We made it just over a kilometer in a back alley of the village before the heat became so intense, my body strained to move under the weight of my equipment. The sun made it feel as if my brain was baking in a convection oven. Very soon, I found myself having to think through putting one foot in front of the other. As I struggled mentally to control my fatigued body, I had to remain extremely vigilant and tactical, mindful that, as Bandit discovered a week prior, this village could erupt dangerously without notice.

We neared the end of the alley, a T-intersection with a wadi (an Afghan irrigation canal). As we halted at the T-intersection, I looked at the desperation on my guy's faces and quickly made the decision to order a short halt. I instructed the guys to post up against a wall that ran parallel to the wadi. As I radioed my commander to inform him of our situation, our platoon medic, Sergeant Dade, drew my attention to Private Van Slyke, who had collapsed. The guys immediately moved him to flat ground, and Dade began his initial care. Van Slyke was still conscious, saying "I can go on, I can go on." A tough, proud twenty-year-old kid, neither he nor any one of us knew how dire his situation would become.

I radioed my commander that we had a possible heat casualty. As I uttered those words through the squawk box of my radio, Dade, once again drew my attention. Within seconds, Van Slyke had completely crashed. He had become totally unresponsive and sweat was beginning to crystalize on his face. I looked at his lifeless, ghost white, purple face, and knew we had to get him out immediately. I started thinking through how we were going to do it.

I quickly decided we should move back out to an open field I had noticed when we walked in. I knew it would be suitable for a Blackhawk MEDEVAC helicopter. I took two of my guys with me, Specialist Moore and Private Stewart. I left Dade to continue to administer aid to Van Slyke, as Sergeant Robinson and Sergeant McInnis pulled security. This was still a seriously hostile area. If the Taliban had chosen to fight at that moment, with us inwardly consumed in caring for one of our own rather than outwardly focused on the surrounding danger, I have no doubt we could have been overrun, captured, or killed. Nevertheless, we reached the open field just in time. I nearly collapsed to the ground when I took a knee. At that point, the only reason my body was continuing to function was because it had to, mentally.

Totally winded and exhausted, I spoke into my squawk box, "Hellraiser Main, this is Jester 6, I have a 9-line MEDEVAC request." (In Army culture, when the words "9-line MEDEVAC" go out over the radio, everyone shuts up and listens.)

"Jester 6, this is Hellraiser Main, send your 9-line, over."

Without hesitation, I responded with labored breaths, "Line 1, location." I paused, looking down at my Garmin GPS wristband, "mike sierra five, eight, three, zero, niner, eight, four, zero."

I sent the remaining eight lines of the MEDEVAC request format detailing the patient battle roster number and condition. Within minutes, Dade, McInnis, and Robinson appeared out of the alley with Van Slyke. Unknown to me, as I was sending up the MEDEVAC request, back at their location in Shewan, Van Slyke's condition had worsened (if that was even possible).

These guys are truly rare individuals. Though the majority of my men did not know Jesus, I saw the character of God manifested in them time and time again. It was a literal reminder that we truly are all made in the image of God.

They had to cut his uniform completely off, exposing his naked body. All the while, they were taking their personal CamelBak water reservoirs and dumping their contents on his body. Imagine this. In the midst of plus 140-degree heat, sacrificing your only life source—water—for another's life. These guys are truly rare individuals. Though the majority of my men did not know Jesus, I saw the character of God manifested in them time and time again. It was a literal reminder that we truly are all made in the image of God.

They looked like the Country Bear Jamboree, struggling out of Shewan, diligently trying to control Van Slyke's naked, lifeless body, while balancing his gear, equipment, and weapon. It was extremely admirable and heroic (and would later become a source of comedic relief amongst the guys).

The Blackhawk MEDEVAC touched down in a tornado of dust and rotor wash. With the assistance of the in-flight medic, we placed Van Slyke on the stretcher and loaded him on the floor of the MEDEVAC. We all turned our backs from the Blackhawk as the pilots throttled up the rotor. Dust, dirt and debris filled the air like the Dust Bowl during the Great Depression of the 1930s. We all moved back to Shewan Garrison, never having moved further than a kilometer into the village we were supposed to clear behind our sister company, Bandit. Back inside the garrison, we immediately reported to the aid station.

Spent

I laid down on a stretcher as a medic prepared an IV. I was physically, mentally, and emotionally exhausted. Never before had my body experienced what it just had. If a tachometer had been attached to my chest, it would have been pegged all the way into the red. I took the first of six IV bags in a matter of seconds, finishing off all six within five minutes. The medic refused to give me anymore because she said my bloodstream would be too diluted.

My heart went out to Van Slyke, one of my favorite soldiers, and one I had been focused on, spiritually. The night before we deployed, he had accompanied me to "theMill," the college ministry, a part of New Life Church in Colorado Springs. I had shared Joshua 3:5 with him and urged him to consecrate himself in preparation for the deployment.

In the aftermath of the operation, I was personally attacked by my chain of command for the events that transpired on the ground with Van Slyke. As an officer, and particularly as a platoon leader, I am ultimately responsible for everything the platoon does or fails to do. The fact that Van Slyke went down as a severe heat casualty, literally minutes from irreversible brain damage (as we would come to find out), was ultimately pinned on me. Their reasoning was, I must not have adequately prepared my men for the rigors of ground combat in the Afghan environment.

This took a serious toll on me. I knew that my men were hydrated, just as I was. However, at a certain point, water consumption is no longer a factor due to the sheer heat and exposure to the sun. Any of us could have easily been Van Slyke, and probably would have been, had it not been for him going down, and us needing to remain in it to care for the "man down." In the days following the operation, I was grateful to find that Van Slyke was alright. However, I was hurt, and I felt I was at a distance from God.

Back to Farah

The day after our brutal introduction to Afghanistan, we loaded up our trucks and made the hour drive back down South to FOB Farah, our home. The platoon was joyful, as we were looking forward to returning to our own space and stuff. The guys' wives and families had slowly been sending them out an assortment of TVs, Xboxes, PS3s and the like, and the guys were all ready to get back, relax, and enjoy a little bit of home away from home.

In the wake of the incursion into Shewan, the entirety of my platoon was disgusted with Battalion's leadership, lack of planning, and consideration for the effects of initiating such an operation so late in the afternoon. This was the first time I had to be political as far as how I handled the guys, the chain of command, and my own emotions surrounding the operation. Truthfully, I thought it was horrible planning, and that my platoon had been an expendable proponent of someone's flawed vision for our mission in Afghanistan.

I struggled to deal with my own anger surrounding the situation, while still maintaining the "drink the Kool Aid," "toe the party line" leadership posture that doesn't show frustration in front of the men, modeling unflagging support for the chain of command. I knew this to be important for leaders. The guys don't need another complainer, they need someone to stand. *What kind of Christian would I be in front of them, if I was to completely collapse and voice my feelings?* I thought to myself. I bottled it up.

Something's Got to Give

July was evolving into the worst month of my life. I knew we would be busy, and I knew, from previous experience, that a deployment would require a certain level of flexibility and patience. But every day, thus far, we had been outside the wire for something. We were getting spun-up (Army term for responding to a situation) on a daily basis while tasked with quick reaction force. Missions were lasting in excess of twelve hours, in some cases, eighteen.

Unbelievably, during this period, I had somehow managed to cultivate an inappropriate relationship with a female officer on Farah. She was not a Christian, and I had no business pursuing her, but I found myself sneaking off to remote areas of the base with her on the nights that we were not outside the wire.

It was no surprise that, during this time, my walk with Christ was severely neglected. My quiet times had been all but nonexistent. When I did read and seek the Lord, it was unfulfilling because I was unrepentant. I had slowly forgotten the joy I felt on the airplane coming over, when I looked forward to the discipleship opportunities of this deployment. I had neglected the hearts of my men. I was totally self-consumed, unrepentant, and like Jonah, was running to Tarsus, spiritually.

On the outside, I looked good. I didn't cuss, didn't engage in the disreputable conversations of my peers, prayed before eating, and guarded my eyes from the things others were looking at. On the inside, however, I had an insurmountable mountain of pride. I was angry and bitter. I looked like a Pharisee and not at all like Jesus. Little did I know, however, God was getting ready to make His point clear.

The Mission

I walked into our company office to check the patrol schedule and begin working on CONOPs for the upcoming week. My commander had scheduled a patrol of Sur, a village North of Farah city, off of Route 517. In my initial map recon of the village, I noted that it was one of the larger settlements in our area of operations. I began the planning process by logging into Tiger Net, an interactive server for the Armed Services in Afghanistan, to obtain detailed imagery of the village and find any previously documented information from past patrols into the village. The imagery confirmed my earlier suspicions. This village was, in fact, very large. It would prove to be a planning headache.

Zooming in on the center of the village, I plotted a route that we would walk within the village in order to gain atmospherics (patterns of life within the village) before we made contact with the Shurah leader. Taking note of the many alleyways and blind corners of our route, I knew this village would not be one within which an unfamiliar force would want to find itself engaged in a firefight. Nonetheless, for half a day, I sat at the computer and worked diligently to develop a detailed plan I felt comfortable with.

In my research, I discovered that two years before, an element had in fact visited Sur without incident, even noting that the village, largely an agricultural community, was friendly to their presence. This revelation put my previous concerns at ease. From that point, I no longer viewed the patrol as potentially dangerous. I couldn't have been more wrong.

Chapter 4

I DIDN'T EXPECT A FIGHT

"For the weapons of our warfare are not carnal but mighty in God for pulling down strongholds."

2 Corinthians 10:4 *(NKJV)*

14 July 2011

With vehicles and equipment prepared, the platoon huddled up behind our trucks for the patrol brief. Standing in full gear, the platoon listened while I delivered the mission statement. "MP platoon conducts mounted and dismounted patrol to Sur Village no later than 14, 1400, July 2011 in order to conduct a key leader engagement with the Shurah leader and gain atmospherics on the village." I proceeded to describe the mission down to the most minute detail. I covered, in depth, our communication plan, our medical evacuation plan, where our trucks would be placed when we dismounted them at the village, the formation we would use while dismounted and moving through the village, and our action plan for contact with the enemy. At the conclusion of the brief, I said, "Guys, anything could happen, but I don't think anything will." I left it at that and we mounted our vehicles for our fateful trip to Sur village. I did not pray.

When I reflect back on the hour preceding our mission that day, I wonder how I could have been so cavalier, not expecting a fight. There we were, in Afghanistan, in the middle of the fighting season, and we had already seen a good deal of enemy activity. In retrospect, I have no idea why I would think this, or any other mission, did not deserve a high level of alertness.

This applies to Christian living as well, there is no difference. Every day, when we leave the sanctuary of our homes, we are moving forward from our friendly lines into enemy territory. Yet many of us do not truly expect, nor are we prepared, for a fight.

Every day, when we leave the sanctuary of our homes, we are moving forward from our friendly lines into enemy territory. Yet many of us do not truly expect, nor are we prepared, for a fight.

Sure, we know life is life, and at its core, we are broken and sinful people living in a broken and fallen world, but do we approach each day ready to make contact with our enemy and battle him? Many of us have heard, "The thief comes only to steal and kill and destroy," (John 10:10, *ESV*), yet we don't actually expect that to happen each day we back the car out of our driveways.

Furthermore, 1 Peter 5:8 says, "Be self-controlled and alert. Your enemy the devil prowls around like a roaring lion looking for someone to devour." Listen to that, "looking for someone to devour." Does that sound like an enemy we can neglect? An enemy about whom we can claim, "I don't think anything will happen?" Or worse yet, how can we read that and not even pray? It is one thing to pray to God, ask Him to go before you and place a hedge of protection from the evil one around you, and then to step out into a brutal world, with confidence. However, it is totally the opposite thing to not expect a fight with an enemy we know has come to steal, kill, destroy, and ultimately devour us—and to not even pray.

Live a Life on Amber

In the Army, we have several levels of weapon conditions. Weapon status green: the weapon is locked and cleared of ammunition. Weapon status red: the weapon is locked and loaded. Weapon status amber: the weapon is loaded but not locked. In Afghanistan, our weapons were to be set at status amber when we rolled. The magazine is in the magazine well. For the weapon to be changed to red condition requires only a simple pull on the charging handle, which instantly slams a round into the chamber.

What if we lived our lives on amber? What if we lived each day loaded and able to be locked in a second—instantly ready to engage the enemy at hand? Unfortunately, many Christians live their lives as if there is not a battle at hand. Many of us, spiritually, are at weapon status green, meaning, we are neither locked nor loaded.

In order to be spiritually locked, we must know the Word. In order to be loaded, that Word must be on our tongue. When the Word is on our tongue, it can quickly be used to put Satan in his rightful place—under the authority of Christ. When we live our lives on amber, the Word is upon us. No matter the temptation or trial, that Word is readily available to declare, "He who is in you is greater" (1 John 4:4, *ESV*).

Jesus told Peter that he would betray the Son of God, the very man whom Peter abandoned everything to follow. Jesus was preparing him for a future in which a hard decision would have to be made. Yet when the time arrived for Peter to stand and fight for his Savior, he failed to see the reality before him. It was not until he heard the crow of the rooster that Peter realized just how unprepared he had been. As Peter's memory recounted the words of Jesus, the Bible says that Peter "wept bitterly" (Matthew 26:75). This verse serves as a stark reminder that Peter did not want to fail his Savior, his friends, nor himself. It is clear from this scripture that Peter truly did not expect this fight. He did not expect that, in the moment of truth, a fight would be at hand.

I wonder if we, as believers in the one true God, truthfully lived in a way that embraced the gravity of Ephesians 6. It may seem noble and righteous for us to say, "put on the full armor of God," but do we truly expect to encounter an altercation that is not of this world? The point is this: we are heirs to a throne, born into a war—a fight as old as time. Satan is jealous of our standing with God. His goal and aim is to keep us from our inheritance, and because of this, Paul was prompted to illustrate just *who* our struggle is truly against: "For our struggle is not against flesh and blood, but against the rulers, against the authorities, against the powers of this dark world and against the spiritual forces of evil in the heavenly realms" (Ephesians 6:12).

Chapter 5

DECEIVED

"...who exchanged the truth of God for the lie, and worshiped and served the creature rather than the Creator, who is blessed forever. Amen."

Romans 1:25 *(NKJV)*

The current policy regarding U.S. ground forces in Afghanistan is to develop, train and mentor the Afghan national forces, or Afghan National Police (ANP). This has become the focus, since it is inevitable that United States military forces will leave Afghanistan one day, replaced by a legitimate Afghan force capable of providing security and preventing regimes like the Taliban from seizing control of the country again.

Afghan National Police

During our orientation to our area of responsibility, I was introduced to one of the many ANP forces my platoon would partner with. These ANP forces belonged to a reserve battalion, known in Afghanistan as Kandak. The Kandak headquarters was situated only two miles from FOB Farah, so on many missions, we would simply pull in and round up a patrol to accompany us.

Afghanistan is seriously underdeveloped, as you have likely seen on countless news reports. Many protocols followed in the United States to select individuals to perform in civil service positions simply do not exist in Afghanistan. There is no formal census there, no governmental accountability or oversight, and no background information on individuals. The process the Afghan Government uses to recruit and select candidates for service is largely based on trust or tribal affiliation, and in most cases, is mired in corruption. Aware of this, we were always very cautious, almost to the point of distrusting ANP members when we trained or operated with them. However, policy mandated that on any patrol, the ANP presence would be first and last, with U.S. forces in the middle. This was to create the impression amongst the local population that Afghan forces were "in charge" and "capable."

Colonel Baboo

Sur village was the largest village in our area of operations. Meeting with the village Shurah leader was an essential task in order for us to determine the village's security concerns and overall view on Afghan National Security Forces. En route to the village, we stopped at the Kandak headquarters. I found the commander, Colonel Baboo, and asked if they would join us on our patrol to the village. Colonel Baboo was a big flour sack of a man. A well-groomed, silver beard sat atop a healthy waistline. He was a bear hugger, and I always tried to evade the inevitable, oxygen-sucking hugs—to no avail. He agreed to offer his forces to partner with us on the patrol.

Within minutes, two ANP trucks—loaded with armed ANP in the bed—were ready to roll out. I briefly covered the mission and route with the ANP commander while Reza, my interpreter, translated. Once I was comfortable with his understanding of the mission, we loaded back up into our trucks. With the ANP vehicles at the front and rear of my patrol, we collectively proceeded through Farah city and up Route 517 to Sur village.

The Man with the Red Hat

The distance between the Kandak and Sur village requires roughly a thirty minute drive. We flew up the highway in our trucks, hanging on for dear life, shooting in and out of traffic, trying to keep up with the ANP as they led us to Sur. Just as in most underdeveloped countries, driving in Afghanistan was a dicey endeavor.

Upon arrival, we pulled into the open field behind a school UNICEF had built, relieved that we had survived the drive. With the trucks in place on the road leading into Sur, our dismounted patrol—including our ANP counterparts—prepared for the trek in.

As we positioned ourselves for the dismounted movement, I noticed one of the ANP who was going to be on point for us, was wearing a bright red baseball cap. I briefly thought it was funny and dismissed it. (One of the things we had come to expect from the ANP was their inability to maintain uniformity.) Then I noticed the man was anxious and, at the time, seemed nervous. I was by no means an expert in Afghan personalities or dynamics, so I didn't read too much into his demeanor. Besides, the mission at hand was largely concerned with getting into Sur and making contact with the Shurah leader, so again, I dismissed it.

The man walked at the very front of our formation, red hat shining in the sunlight. My trust, for better or worse, was firmly in the hands of the ANP, particularly in the red-capped man my men and I trailed into Sur.

The Wrong Way

Judas was an ally to Jesus, much as the ANP were allied to us. Jesus placed His trust in Judas. And even in light of knowing that Judas would eventually betray Him, Jesus loved and mentored Judas. Judas embraced Jesus in the Garden of Gethsemane, even betraying him with a kiss that identified Him to His enemies. This was quickly followed by armed conflict in which Jesus was arrested and ultimately, turned over to death.

The man in the red hat had initially embraced me with a handshake and, typical of Afghani culture, even placed his hand over his heart after we shook. This same man was now leading us down a canalized path, deep into the heart of Sur village. As I checked my wrist GPS during our movement, I realized that the ANP were directing us down a route I had not intended to take, according to my mission planning. On my right side, we passed the path that I originally plotted for our movement into Sur. In that moment, I thought to myself: *This is the wrong way.* Although I was aware we were taking the wrong direction into the village, I decided not to adjust our route. I trusted the ANP leading us, so my platoon continued following them towards what we would soon find to be a fatal alleyway.

Following a Lie

As Christians, we know that Satan is a deceiver, schemer, and liar; yet, we follow. Blinded by whatever it is we are placing our trust in (which isn't God), we continue on a path we know is wrong. The enemy appeals to our trust, using it to lead us astray. I trusted in the ANP that day. While following them, I knew it was the wrong way, but in light of the trust I was to have in them, I continued anyway.

When Christians misplace their trust, it allows Satan to work his destructive plan. When we place our trust in anyone or anything except God, Satan uses it to lead us down the wrong route. Unbeknownst to me, I was following a lie that day. Unbeknownst to many of us, this is also the case when we are out of step with Jesus. We walk the lie until it is ultimately met with trouble. In each individual life, the lie can look very different, but the end state is the same—destruction.

As Christians, we know that Satan is a deceiver, schemer, and liar; yet, we follow. Blinded by whatever it is we are placing our trust in (which isn't God), we continue on a path we know is wrong. The enemy appeals to our trust, using it to lead us astray.

Judas followed the lie of riches and it led him right up to the cheek of Jesus, to betray Him. Ultimately, Judas hung himself under the shame of his betrayal of Jesus for a few pieces of silver. Judas had experienced the miracles and seen Jesus (God in flesh) perform the impossible. He knew Jesus' divinity, without a doubt. Unfortunately, Judas allowed himself to be deceived. He trusted riches, not Jesus, to be the answer to whatever he aspired for himself. Satan was right there, speaking lies into his ear, and it led to murder of the innocent and suicide of the deceived.

When our trust is rooted in something other than Jesus, Satan is right there with one hand on our back and the other stretched out, leading us down the path to destruction.

I had been deceived; literally walking out the lie that these men were our allies. My trust, and the lives of my men, now relied on the deplorable unseen intentions of these betrayers. Jesus is calling us to trust solely in Him and Him alone. When our trust is rooted in something other than Jesus, Satan is right there with one hand on our back and the other stretched out, leading us down the path to destruction. Whatever the path may be, it ends in one place—trouble. We were about to be in that place, in the greatest trouble of our lives.

Staff Sergeant Parks, outside an ANP checkpoint.

On patrol in Shewan, July 10, 2011.

Post soccer match at the Farah soccer fields.

The Oshkosh MAT-V.

My interpreter, Reza, and I before mission.

Overlooking Farah city.

From right to left: Sergeant Lambert, Staff Sergeant Parks, and I before patrol in downtown Farah.

From left to right: First Sergeant Larsen, Sergeant Robinson and I, standing at the intersection in Sur village, several days after the ambush. Further down the alleyway behind us is where the ambush occurred.

Maneuvering the MAT-Vs outside FOB Farah.

Patrolling the outskirts of Farah city.

The village mosque in Sur, behind an open field. This field ran parallel to the alleyway. We took heavy fire from the mosque on 14 July 2011.

My platoon's 1st squad at Shindand Air Base before our move to Delaram in April, 2012, two months before returning to the United States.

Chapter 6

HE KNEW SOMETHING
I DIDN'T

"...who comforts us in all our troubles, so that we can comfort those in any trouble with the comfort we ourselves have received from God."

2 Corinthians 1:4

There were twelve of us in total, and we staggered ourselves on opposite sides of the road. We kept a distance of at least ten feet between each man. This is doctrinal, and is meant to negate the enemy's ability to kill or wound multiple soldiers in an ambush, based on distance. Reza, my interpreter and I were in the middle, where I could effectively command and control our movement down the barren road and into the village.

Moving In

It was miserably hot, at least 140 degrees—just as it had been in Shewan. And again, each one of us carried in excess of eighty pounds. Pasted to our chests was our IOTV, the body armor that carries a front, back, and two side plates which protect the vital organs of the torso. (Although the IOTV was a huge improvement over previous vests, it was still uncomfortable and heavy.) Strapped to the body armor were eleven magazines of thirty rounds of concrete piercing 5.56mm ammunition, one fragmentation grenade, two smoke grenades, two star clusters (a firework, used as a signal device), a radio, and a CamelBak. I had my 9mm sidearm strapped to my leg and my M4 assault rifle in my hands.

It is hard to imagine, even having done it, how it is possible to function under the weight of all those essential items, especially in that oppressive heat. You can literally feel the sweat beads cascade down your back like Niagara Falls. I learned early on to wear a bandana under my helmet like Deion Sanders; otherwise the sweat would just pour from my head down onto my face, the salt concentrated precipitation stinging my eyes. In all, between the heat and carrying the gear, it was just miserable. We have a saying in the Army: "Embrace the suck." So, we embraced it and moved West into Sur in a staggered column formation.

The Boy

As we walked in, our weapons at the low ready and heads on a swivel, a fourteen or fifteen-year-old boy on my left, walking in the opposite direction, caught my attention. Fairly tall for his young age, slender, with bushy black hair, his face dark from a lifetime spent in the sun, and deep, dark brown eyes—there was something eerie about the way he walked. I locked eyes with him. As we did, he nonverbally communicated that he knew something I didn't.

In hindsight, I should have halted the movement and taken my interpreter with me to speak to him. He knew what we were walking into. And even if he was only an accomplice, something about his demeanor (and no doubt, his story), would have alerted me to an imminent threat.

Paul charged Timothy with carrying the church in Ephesus forward. Imagine if Timothy had never reached out to Paul (or vice versa). Every Timothy needs a Paul, and every Paul needs a Timothy. This is especially true in our lives as Christians today. How can we expect to be prepared for battle when we have no one with whom to inquire that knows about the battle? Worse yet, what if we have knowledge of the battle, yet fail to share it with others who are unprepared?

How can we expect to be prepared for battle when we have no one with whom to inquire that knows about the battle? Worse yet, what if we have knowledge of the battle, yet fail to share it with others who are unprepared?

When I first became a Christian, I was invited to live in an intentional living house with other, more seasoned Christian guys. In that instance, I was the Timothy, and collectively, they were the Paul. Had I not taken their offer to move in and be held accountable, and had I not been open to discipleship, I might not be writing these words today. The Bible features a great many people who have gone before us, that tried to survive on their own, failed, and inevitably sought God and other believers to succeed. This is an example we cannot dismiss or neglect.

In the Army, we refer to this as having a "battle buddy." Battle buddies are simply two soldiers who are friends in uniform, and due to the nature of their friendship, there is little they won't do for one another. Your battle buddy is the guy who is going to stay beside you when the enemy rounds are coming in.

Your battle buddy is the guy who is going to stay beside you when the enemy rounds are coming in.

We need this in the Body of Christ—buddies who are going through the rigors of combat against Satan and sin.

We need this in the Body of Christ—buddies who are going through the rigors of combat against Satan and sin. We need people we can count on to be there when we encounter it ourselves. These are the guys and girls you want to stop and talk to before you continue your movement into one of life's many "unknown villages."

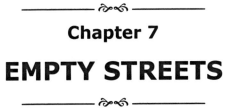

Chapter 7

EMPTY STREETS

"But we have the mind of Christ."

1 Corinthians 2:16

As we moved further into the village, one thing became abundantly clear: we were alone. The village was dead silent, resembling an Old West ghost town that time had forsaken. My immediate realization was that there were no children. I have been all over the world, and the one commonality between third world, undeveloped countries is the abundance of children.

No Kids

Even in the short time we had been in Afghanistan, one thing was clear; when we were on patrol, the children were right beside us. The children of Afghanistan were pretty consistent with those I had seen in Iraq, India, Haiti, and Honduras—they cling to you like glue. We learned pretty quickly that a sure way to incite a riot was to start passing out candy, water, or any other handout.

During one of our first missions in Afghanistan, we mistakenly began handing out Gatorade from one of our trucks. Within seconds, I was sure that our fourteen-ton

Oshkosh vehicle was going to be picked up and pushed over by the mob of children. It was intense! This in mind, I knew the absence of children was uncharacteristic. Again, this should have been a warning sign to me to halt our movement and reevaluate the way we were going about visiting this village. Unfortunately, I didn't draw the correlation between the absence of the kids and the potential for danger.

Something Different About Us

The reason the kids were so attracted to our patrols was because we were different from anything they had ever seen before. In their bleak existence of sun, agriculture, and oppression, the children were easily attracted to anything foreign to the world they knew. We were different. We were taller, had things they knew we would give them, and were decked out with equipment that appeals to the interests of children. Sound familiar? As Christians, we should attract nonbelievers around us because of the difference that having Christ within us makes in our lives.

As Christians, we should attract nonbelievers around us because of the difference that having Christ within us makes in our lives.

Early in our deployment, I noticed a municipal soccer field near FOB Farah. Late in the afternoons, as we returned to base, I noticed numerous kids of various ages all gathered at this soccer field, playing the game they love most. I thought to myself, *How awesome would it be if we were to show up there one afternoon to watch, or better, play with them?* I pitched the idea to my commander, and he was quick to get on board. Even though we viewed the event through two different lenses, mine from a position of love, and his from public relations, nonetheless, he authorized the "patrol" to go the soccer field to observe or play.

Late in the afternoon on one very hot, summer day, we rolled out of FOB Farah, en route to the soccer fields. Just as I anticipated, many children were there, playing. I instructed my interpreter, Reza, to go and coordinate it with the kids to allow us to jump in, and he did. Within minutes, we had identified captains, and were picking teams. Two Afghani boys stood there in front of their friends alongside my soldiers, and commenced to take turns selecting their teams. Each team had an equal number of Afghani boys and soldiers.

Even though we were not in a secured area (downtown Farah city, essentially), we stripped off all our gear. Gone were the cumbersome body armor, ammo, helmets, and weapons. Through God's sovereign protection, none of us were picked off by a sniper rifle amidst our quasi World Cup. It was simply us in multi-cam uniforms and boots, running around on the field of play.

You should know that Afghani kids are incredible at soccer, and made us look like fools. I felt as if I was playing a team full of Pele's. They darted in and out of us like we were statues. At times, it felt as if we were in one of the *Matrix* movies. It was an incredible experience for all of us. My soldiers experienced a mission trip, even if they weren't followers of Jesus Christ.

At one point, I took a breather, desperately in need of it. I stood there, drawing oxygen into my lungs, watching my men and the Afghani children sharing laughter and joy. Together, they were running around the field, passing the ball back and forth—and scoring. It was one of the most joyful times of my life.

After what seemed like an eternity, we concluded the game with a quick speech and took a picture with the Afghanis we had played with. I spoke to the children as Reza interpreted for me. I told them we were neighbors; we lived right up the road from the very field we were standing on. I made the point that we were no different from them; that beneath the body armor and helmets we were human beings, same as them. Finally, I thanked them and told them to never be afraid to come and visit with us when they saw us out and around their city.

Our hearts are in line with Christ's when we are in Him.

I can honestly declare, without pride, that my platoon was most likely the first in the history of U.S. ground forces involved in Afghanistan to pull up to an Afghani soccer field, strip off our protective gear, and play a pickup game in the downtown of a crowded Afghani city. If I wasn't a Christian, I would never have seen the point in that. Our hearts are in line with Christ's when we are in Him. This is why, as Christians, we do the things we do for others. "If then you have been raised with Christ, seek the things that are above, where Christ is, seated at the right hand of God" (Colossians 3:1, *ESV*).

Cities on a Hill

In the Sermon on the Mount, Jesus told us: "You are the light of the world. A city on a hill cannot be hidden" (Matthew 5:14). When I think of this verse, I get the picture of a lost wanderer, a man who is cold, rejected and broken, stumbling into a dark city. All he wants is to find shelter from the elements and help, both physical and physiological. He moves down the main street of the town, the night so dark he can hardly make out the outlines of the dwellings around him. The sliver of hope the man had to find help when he first entered the town quickly fades as he realizes there is none to be found. So he continues to walk, every fiber of muscle strained from weeks, days and years of wandering. The weight of the world has been upon his shoulders, forcing his head and neck towards the ground. As the street comes to an end, and hope is all but lost, the man pauses as a single glimmer of light penetrates the dark cold night. He looks up toward the heavens, and seated atop a hill that rises above the sleeping town, he sees a home with a single welcoming light. As he approaches, the light seems to burn brighter and brighter as he focuses on it through the fog.

"You are the light of the world. A city on a hill cannot be hidden" (Matthew 5:14).

As Christians, that home on the hill is us, and the light burning brighter and brighter is Christ within us. Nothing else can attract the wanderer, the nonbeliever. The light compels them to ascend the hill and cover the distance to the waiting home. When the wanderer arrives, he finds a meal on the table that satisfies his appetite for eternity. This home is a shelter that stands strong amidst the most furious of nature's wrath. There too, he finds rest that brings forth peace which surpasses his understanding.

This home is a shelter that stands strong amidst the most furious of nature's wrath. There too, he finds rest that brings forth peace which surpasses his understanding.

Fruit

Drawing nearer to the heart of Sur, the total lack of any civilian presence was unnerving. Among those of us who had served in the Iraq and Afghanistan campaigns, it was widely known that eerie quietness and little to no civilian presence usually preceded an ambush.

If people are not seeking us out because of the light within us, or conversely, we are not seeking them out in spite of the light within us, it should be unnerving—a sign that we need to reevaluate our current relationship with the Lord.

As Christians, if we have few to no people seeking what we have within us in Jesus, or few to no people we are actively pursuing for Jesus, it is an indicator that we have either been or will be ambushed by the enemy. Jesus said,

"By their fruit you will recognize them" (Matthew 7:20). My friend, the bottom line is this: If people are not seeking us out because of the light within us, or conversely, we are not seeking them out in spite of the light within us, it should be unnerving—a sign that we need to reevaluate our current relationship with the Lord.

Chapter 8

AMBUSHED

"Dear friends, do not be surprised at the painful trial you are suffering, as though something strange were happening to you."

1 Peter 4:12

We turned a corner. The man with the red hat was still leading the formation from the front. At this point, the fact that the boy had given me the suspicious look, the fact that we were clearly being led in a way I had not intended, and the fact of a total absence of children had reached the tipping point of sure negligence on my part. Subconsciously, I knew something was awry, however, I was so focused on finding the Shurah leader and conducting my KLE (Key Leader Engagement) that I was oblivious to the hazards and danger that were afoot.

We began moving down an alleyway that was, at the most, seven feet across, bordered on the left and right by earthen walls, approximately five feet high. From my training, doctrinally, I knew this was canalized terrain, the ideal setting for ambushing an unsuspecting victim. Still following, though against my better judgment, my platoon and I proceeded.

After moving forward for what seemed to be a football field's distance, I finally radioed up to my point man who was just behind the man with the red hat.

"Jester 1-1, this is Jester 6. The first Afghani you see, stop. I am going to come forward with the interpreter to find out where exactly we can find this Shurah leader."

"Roger, Jester 6," Jester 1-1 acknowledged. (He was one of my seasoned team leaders, Sergeant McInnis.)

After a few more steps, sure enough, the deception had run its course. Against my better judgment, following the man with the red hat and continuing on the wrong route behind him, inevitably led us right into the clutches of trouble. We approached another alleyway that formed a T-intersection with the one we were walking down. At that point, with their objective complete, the man with the red hat and his ANP peers sprinted away from us to the North.

Contact!

Suddenly, an RPG (Rocket Propelled Grenade) zoomed by from the intersecting alleyway and into the earthen wall to the right of us. Instantly, a massive orange explosion engulfed everything around us. The sound and explosion sent a concussive wave through our formation that flung us violently against the left wall. With smoke still billowing from the explosion, I saw my men that had been up near the front running back towards me, spilled out against the wall.

In the midst of the chaos, I noticed one of my soldiers, Sergeant Keltner, had a gaping wound on his arm.

He took up a position behind me, and I inspected his arm. Blood was gushing out. I knew it was bad, but he would make it. I called our medic, Sergeant Dade, forward to tend to it.

Instantly, small arms fire erupted all around us from an orchestra of Russian made Kalashnikov AK-47 assault rifles and RPK light machine guns. This was bad. Sergeant Dade had sprinted from the rear of the formation to our position at the front and pulled Sergeant Keltner back to stop the bleeding and dress the wound. I knew we needed to return fire immediately.

A firefight is like a football game. If the quarterback is picking your defensive secondary apart, it is usually because he has no pressure to contend with. However, as soon as your defense applies pressure right in his face, his throws become more hurried and errant. The same principle applies in direct fire combat. The enemy had free reign to fire on us, unimpeded and effectively, until we fired back in his direction.

I shouted for my machine gunner, Specialist Thomas, to come forward: "Thomas! Give me a base of fire to the front, NOW!" Thomas bounded forward with the heaviest firepower we had on the ground, the M240 Bravo, a behemoth of a machine gun. Fired by one person, it is capable of unleashing nearly a thousand rounds per minute. Thomas ran up, and in one fluid motion, dropped it in place, assumed a prone position behind it, and began dumping rounds back to the North: BOOM! BOOM! BOOM! BOOM! BOOM! the 240 rang out. This afforded me a few precious seconds to think.

He Spoke

You would think that in those precious seconds I would have been able to formulate some semblance of a plan. Wrong. Two things occurred to me. The first was that two years prior, I was in Intermediate Spanish II on the University of Arkansas campus, and now, I was being shot at. The second: God said, "This is not the place to ignore me."

God doesn't author evil, but He can usher redemption through it! And while I was glued to the wall, with rounds hissing and popping all around me, God was able to reach into that moment and speak to me because He loves me. Up to that moment, I had defaulted on my calling for this season of my life: to walk in righteousness before my men, proclaim the goodness of God, and seek Him in this dark place. I was delinquent on all three of those things. God was using one of the most horrific experiences of my life to call me out.

God doesn't author evil, but He can usher redemption through it! And while I was glued to the wall, with rounds hissing and popping all around me, God was able to reach into that moment and speak to me because He loves me.

I have seen this repeatedly throughout my walk as a Christian, most notably, when I went to Haiti in the wake of the catastrophic earthquake that struck the island in January, 2010. During my week there, I was blown away by the many testimonies I heard from Haitians of God working both during and after the earthquake to bring them to

Christ. In a culture that is about as far from Jesus as any can possibly get, He alone was the shining beacon of hope and light in the darkness of the aftermath of that natural disaster. Nothing stood except the cross and the work Jesus accomplished on it.

God was using one of the most horrific experiences of my life to call me out.

Christians, we are not exempt from anything in this world. In fact, we are probably exposed to more because of our faith and the attention from Satan it attracts. God is not the author of evil. However, we live in a sinful, fallen, and evil world. Because of this, we need to realize that when evil comes, God, in His infinite sovereignty, can and will work through it to bring forth His good and loving purposes. After much reflection on this, I believe that God saw the danger I, His adopted son, was in. Helpless and afraid, pinned down against a wall in Afghanistan, I said to myself: *This is defining. This is sustainable. This is a revelation.*

Think of Paul, on his way to Damascus to murder Christians, with an aim to put an end to a movement of love and redemption. Recall that he was temporarily blinded. From that moment would come the definition of a man, the sustainability of his existence, and the revelation of a life. From there, Paul proceeded to advance the Kingdom of Jesus Christ, in light of his past. I know the Kingdom of Jesus Christ is advanced in the same way, in light of our past and the evil that comes upon us!

An Invisible Enemy

We were in the fight of our lives. It was happening, and it was happening now. Rounds were coming in with an almost indescribable frequency. They were slamming into the dirt around our boots, the wall we were completely exposed against, and passing between us. At one point, I was giving direction to one of my sergeants, our faces just inches apart, when a round passed between our noses. Dirt and wall fragments sprayed around us as if they were being jack-hammered. Dust filled the air and the sound of my men shouting back and forth strained to rise over the deafening sound of the abundant automatic weapon fire.

Through all of this, I was vigorously trying to identify an enemy target to which my men could direct fire. I identified cardinal directions, and directed fire in those areas, but I could not identify one single Taliban fighter. The enemy was literally invisible. They were so dug in and concealed that it was impossible to spot them. Meanwhile, we were taking fire from our left, front, and right sides. They had us dead to rights, and it is only by God's grace that we are all still here today.

Sound familiar? Satan operates in the same way, and his tactics are just as cowardly. All we can identify is the chaos around us, but he is there, dug in, totally concealed, orchestrating it all.

Popping Smoke

Early on, I had called Staff Sergeant Parks on the radio and frantically told him that we were in contact in the village. Parks, a native of Richmond, Virginia, and a former small forward for the All-Army Europe basketball team, was a true professional. He immediately began relaying our status on the ground back to Battalion headquarters at FOB Farah.

When our situation turned dire in the village and we were unable to identify the enemy, it was clear we were all going to be turned into cherry cobbler if we stayed. We had to pull out of the village. I told Parks we were on our way back to the trucks: "Jester 1, this is Jester 6. We're pulling out. Bring the trucks into the village as close as possible and we'll rally with you there." He acknowledged and I shouted, as best I could, over the fray that we were leaving.

The doctrinal term for falling back is "breaking contact." This is a controlled maneuver that allows soldiers to cover each other's movements as they fall back. Once the first soldier falls back, he takes up a position and covers the other as he falls back, and so on, until all soldiers have reached the designated rally point (in our case, the trucks).

During this maneuver, the use of a smoke grenade is an incredible asset because it conceals your movement. A smoke grenade releases a dense plume of smoke of various colors, and is nearly impossible to see through. You may recall a *Batman* movie, where the Caped Crusader uses smoke to mask his exit. The same principle applies.

I was the last man in our movement out. As my men bounded in buddy teams back, I frantically pulled a red smoke grenade from a utility pouch on my vest and, in practically the same motion, extracted the pin from the grenade. I waited a second or two, due to the delay of the fuse on the grenade (referred to as "cooking it off"), and then underhanded it down the alleyway. As the smoke billowed and filled the entire alleyway, I fired my weapon repeatedly, reloaded the magazine, ran back, and then fired it again.

We made it back to a T-intersection where the man in the red hat had initially turned and led our patrol into the fatal alleyway. We were exhausted from running under the weight of our gear. Our lungs struggled for oxygen due to the constriction of the body armor. At this point, we were still taking heavy enemy fire, and the rounds seemed to be much more accurate. I could see the trucks to the East, but they were still quite a distance away.

I looked at the three soldiers closest to me and wondered if we had the strength to run the rest of the distance. Either way, I knew we would have to run because catty-corner to us was a large open field, a danger area. Moving adjacent to it, we would be fully exposed. At about this time, the Taliban began dropping mortars on us. A mortar is like an artillery shell, an indirect fire weapon meant to drop on you from the sky, enveloping you in a cloud of shrapnel, effectively reducing you to a human slushy.

I shouted to the three men with me, "Get ready to MOVE!" I ran to the middle of the intersection and threw a white smoke grenade in the large open area. As it landed and began to billow, I shouted for the three to go. They passed by me in a flash, drawing on every last ounce of energy and oxygen to make the sprint to the trucks. As they moved, I continued to hug the wall, firing in the direction of a cluster of homes back near the alleyway to cover my men. When the last man cleared the intersection, under cover of the haze of white smoke, I too drew on every last ounce of energy and sprinted to the trucks. I probably ran to the trucks faster than a sprinter in the final heat of the Olympics. If Nike had been there, I am sure I would have received a shoe deal. My adrenaline was red-lined. My heart was ready to take flight out of my chest. No doubt my blood pressure was nearing the point of explosion. Mortars and small arms fire continued to land around us as we covered the distance back to the trucks.

To add insult to injury, over the volley of automatic fire, mortar explosions, and the screaming, I could literally hear the enemy laughing. That hurt. It is no different with Satan. We follow the lie leading to trouble, and in the midst of it, our invisible enemy laughs as we struggle for our lives.

Chapter 9

THE TRUCKS

"The LORD is my rock, my fortress and my deliverer."

2 Samuel 22:2

In the modern-day Army, vehicles are our horses, and there is nothing more muscular and capable than the Oshkosh MAT-V. The MAT-V is a behemoth, period. A massive 12-cylinder diesel Caterpillar engine produces 400 horsepower and yields a whopping one thousand plus pounds of torque. The truck is a beast. Designed with a V-shaped hull to defeat the IED threat, the cabin is shrouded in armor as thick as a log cabin. Inside the vehicle are four seats and a gunner's position. The gunner stands on a platform and operates a crew-served machine gun that can be mounted to the turret.

As the TC (Truck Commander) in the front, right passenger seat, I have an array of assets available to me. Directly in front of me, is the BFT (Blue Force Tracker), a touch screen tablet. Constantly updated from a satellite on the truck, I can see other friendly forces in the area, send them instant messages, and obtain current grid locations to my position and any other position I want to plot on the digital map. To my left, between the driver and I, stands a tower, a green conglomerate of radio equipment. Included in this array of radios one practically needs a PhD to operate, are satellite radios we can use to reach out for assistance anywhere, regardless of distance or terrain. We can also use it to control our electronic countermeasures on board. When operating, the electronic countermeasures, known as the "Duke" after John Wayne, will jam signals the Taliban use via remote to detonate IEDs.

The Oshkosh MAT-V should be featured on History Channel's *Modern Marvels*. It is a far cry from the safari-mobiles we cruised around in back in 2003 when I was deployed to Iraq. The evolution of the modern battlefield demanded the development of such a vehicle. We are blessed to have them, and they are the most physical symbol of power in our platoon. I have said it before, and will say it again: "Thank you, taxpayers."

Armor

When we were deep in the fatal clutches of Sur, I always knew that back at the Oshkosh MAT-V, we had refuge in the form of armor and firepower. The decision I made to break contact out of the village was based solely on the fact that the trucks were the only place we could go to provide safety for my men.

Paul tells us twice in Ephesians 6 to "put on the full armor of God." He does not tell us to put it on halfway or three-quarters of the way; he says all the way. In the fights we find ourselves in as Christians on this earth, we need to be sure that we are donning the full armor of God.

For soldiers in Afghanistan, the MAT-V provides all the armor and protection we need, but if one of the thick windows is cracked, the whole structural integrity is compromised, and its ability to provide effective protection deteriorates severely. Had we rolled into Sur that day in a truck with windows cracked (even from normal wear), and been struck by a mortar or RPG, the potential for penetration would have been very high. Likewise, we would not get the full protection the armor afforded us, if once we reached the trucks, one of the guys was still dismounted, on the ground. There is no halfway; either you are protected or you are not.

Paul tells us twice in Ephesians 6 to "put on the full armor of God." He does not tell us to put it on halfway or three-quarters of the way; he says all the way. In the fights we find ourselves in as Christians on this earth, we need to be sure that we are donning the full armor of God.

At the trucks, my men would be covered with inches of precious armor, and I had enough firepower to level the whole village if I needed to. Clothing ourselves in the full armor of our Lord and Savior, Jesus Christ, means we are fully in. We can't have the door open with one leg dangling out. It literally means we have no other options. There is no other route we can take. We cannot protect ourselves, we need to be harnessed into our seat with the door battle-locked. From there, we can watch the strength and firepower in Jesus unleashed on our enemy.

The Rock

The trucks were our rock, our safe refuge amidst the chaos, and we desperately needed to run to them as fast as possible in the midst of death. In the midst of death, there is no refuge greater than God. Just as dire as the need had been for us to get back to our trucks that miserable afternoon in the heat of July, is the need for us, as Christians, to break contact and get back to our Rock amidst spiritual and physical attacks and circumstances.

In the midst of death, there is no refuge greater than God.

David understood this as clearly as anyone. Throughout his life, David was continually under siege, through Goliath, Saul, numerous foreign armies, Bathsheba, and Absalom. We see David, a man under the most dire of circumstance, running to his Rock—God—who he knew to be his only refuge. We may not see a more clearly written understanding of just who God is amidst trouble than what David wrote of Him in Psalm 18:2: "The Lord is my rock, my fortress and my deliverer; my God is my rock, in whom I take refuge. He is my shield and the horn of my salvation, my stronghold."

Had I ignored the fact that the trucks were there to move my men back to, I might well be living with the death of one or more of my soldiers on my heart and conscience for the rest of my life. Many of my soldiers believed in God, however, they couldn't have been further from walking victoriously in Him. Up to that point, I had neglected the work God called me to do in the Army, particularly among my men in Afghanistan. I do not know if I would have been able to live with myself, had even one of them been killed because I had not acted any sooner in ordering them to break contact, knowing we had the trucks to retreat to.

It would have been very hard not to think that I was personally responsible, having both failed to spend time with them showing them Christ, and protect them in Sur, resulting in their death. After all, I was responsible for them, just as a father is responsible for his family. This was my family, and I was the head. I had the responsibility to live out Jesus to them, and in the midst of the fight, direct them to the rock—the stronghold.

> *We worship God when we abandon ourselves to Him, and forsake our pathetic attempts to weather whatever it is we are facing under our own perceived strength.*

Running to the Rock is ultimately an act of worship. We worship God when we abandon ourselves to Him, and forsake our pathetic attempts to weather whatever it is we are facing under our own perceived strength. Would you agree that our God is a jealous God? If so, then you should agree that attempting to rectify any problem, strife, trouble, or ambush on your own is to attempt to effectively bypass that same jealous God. We worship God with our lives. Every facet, endeavor, and reaction of our existence should ultimately be attributed to the Lord.

> *We worship God with our lives. Every facet, endeavor, and reaction of our existence should ultimately be attributed to the Lord.*

Joshua communicated this when he wrote as a final declaration of his life, "As for me and my family, we'll worship

God" (Joshua 24:15, *MSG*). There is nothing I could have done of my own that day. Neglecting the trucks as our sole refuge in the midst of an unfamiliar place, while facing a hostile enemy, would have no doubt caused the death of one or more of my soldiers. Similarly, if we neglect God as our sole refuge in a hostile land, facing a deadly enemy, we concede to death.

---

if we neglect God as our sole refuge in a hostile land, facing a deadly enemy, we concede to death.

Chapter 10

DEFEAT?

"You therefore must endure hardship as a good soldier of Jesus Christ."

2 Timothy 2:3 (*NKJV*)

It is hard to write what I need to say in this chapter, even now, sixteen months removed from the events I recount here. I have spent many restless nights mulling over the ambush we endured on 14 July 2011, angry and bitter over the way we were attacked, and by the way I was personally criticized by my commander and the Battalion commander. These consumed my heart and mind like a triangle choke in a UFC fight.

Getting Out

Staff Sergeant Parks had hastily maneuvered our trucks to face back towards Route 517, allowing an egress out of Sur. First Sergeant Larsen, Sergeant Robinson, and I, were the last to arrive at the trucks—all gassed. With mortars and automatic fire still erupting all around us, we all but flew into our seats. Our gunners on the trucks manned the heavy .50 caliber machine guns, indiscriminately dumping a volley of armor-piercing rounds back towards Sur—a formidable onslaught of fire.

Over the radio, Staff Sergeant Parks informed me that we were "green 2 green," meaning all our personnel were accounted for. At that update, the words, "Let's go!" couldn't have come off my tongue any quicker. Our drivers stomped their gas pedals through the floorboards, and the massive Caterpillar engines roared to life, digging ruts as a thousand pounds of torque was released to the rear tires. Sergeant Keltner, suffering from the wound on his arm, slipped in and out of consciousness as we owned the road all the way back down South to FOB Farah.

We pulled the trucks into the FOB and drove them straight to the aid station. Staff Sergeant Parks had radioed ahead and informed them that we did have a casualty, so our medical personnel were ready to receive our wounded. While Sergeant Keltner was being attended to, we staged our trucks and left them in a ready status. We were certain we would go back into Sur that night with another platoon to support us.

Second-guessing

My commander sought me out almost immediately upon our return, and he was not pleased. Out of sight of my men, he berated me over the operation. With the failed mission in Shewan still fresh in my mind, I was utterly disgusted that I was, once again, having to explain and justify myself to somebody that wasn't even on the ground with us. To make matters worse, our TOC (Tactical Operations Center) reported that the ANP were still in contact in Sur. To my command, this effectively meant that I had simply abandoned our Afghan National Police counterparts in the city.

Fighting back every raw emotion, and struggling to keep myself in check, I stood there and attempted to explain that we were set up. We had essentially been delivered into the hands of the Taliban on a silver platter by our so-called "allies." In the heat of the moment, neither my commander nor Battalion commander entertained any of it. Of course, neither of them had been on the ground when we were led into the clutches of death by the ANP, nor were they there when I screamed at the ones I could still see to pull back with us. I truly believe that if I had run back into that village, trying to recover the ANP, I would have been shot and killed. And if I had been shot and killed, more of my men would have suffered the same fate trying to recover my body. Furthermore, at that point, I could not distinguish between a potential friendly ANP and an enemy one. I am positive today, just as I was that day while standing there being reprimanded, that there were ANP actually shooting at us as well. I stood there sweating, soliciting every ounce of discipline I had not to lash out. I honestly could not believe that the two officers had expected me, at the expense of my men's lives or my own, to run back into that death trap of a village it had just taken everything we had to slug our way out of.

In the wake of the mission and consequent scolding, I was at a total loss. I didn't speak to anyone—including my men. I hibernated in my room, still reeling from the events of the day and the ensuing scolding from my superiors. I felt alone and abandoned. Without support, I was left to my own devices to try and make sense of the catastrophic event. The perception among my superiors was that I had failed, and was most likely a coward—I had just cut and run. In those grueling, lonely days, I began to embrace the notion that perhaps I had failed, that we had been defeated, and that quite possibly, I wasn't a good leader. Any attempt at sleep failed in itself. I would lie in bed, oppressively reliving the events of that day. I had resigned myself to defeat, and this event had developed into a chronic disease, attacking my emotions and psyche. I was locked in an endless cycle, simply doubting my actions in pulling us out instead of attempting to stay and fight.

Engrained in my mind, were the honorable and valiant images of scores of soldiers pouring off landing craft onto the beaches of Normandy, under apocalyptic German fire. I recalled accounts of heroic soldiers withstanding multiple wounds to save their comrades' lives throughout the history of warfare. My internal dialogue was in high gear: *Am I just a coward? You couldn't see an enemy. Yes, but maybe if I was a better leader, I would have just led an assault towards where I believed the concentration of Taliban to be. What if you had done that? Would one of your soldiers now be dead? It would have been a whole new ball game if somebody went down badly in that alleyway, just trying to get them out would have caused more casualties. Right, but my job is to close with and destroy the enemy.* These were aggressive arguments that played repeatedly on my mind over the days that followed.

The Storm

I had condemned myself to failure and struggled with the idea that maybe I was, in fact, a coward—unfit to lead men. I became ashamed of myself, and for the next year could not escape the weight of the burden I carried from the events of 14 July 2011. By God's grace, these feelings have proven to be temporary. Think of the storm the disciples were in the midst of in Mark 6:48-50 (ESV): "And about the fourth watch of the night he came to them, walking on the sea. He meant to pass by them, but when they saw him walking on the sea they thought it was a ghost, and cried out, for they all saw him and were terrified. But immediately he spoke to them and said, 'Take heart; it is I. Do not be afraid.'"

The key to this verse is the fourth watch. The significance is, in Roman times, Roman soldiers divided the night into four watches, from 6 p.m. to 6 a.m. By the fourth watch, 3 a.m. to 6 a.m., the disciples had already been battling the storm for nine hours. Nine hours! Can you imagine? The Bible doesn't provide details of it, but I wonder what exactly the disciples had resigned themselves to in the throes of that tremendous storm. Was it failure? Was it defeat? Or was it death?

Jesus comes to us when all seems lost, when it seems hopeless, and we feel we are going to drown.

Just as He did for the disciples after they battled the storm for nine hours, Jesus comes to us when all seems lost, when it seems hopeless, and we feel we are going to drown. That's when Jesus shows up. Even when it seems that He can't get there, Jesus gets there. Furthermore, in the storm, amidst the trials of our faith, we can be confident that we are developing perseverance. And in that we know: "Perseverance must finish its work so that you may be mature and complete, not lacking anything" (James 1:4).

Just as with Afghanistan in general, 14 July 2011 is not a day I would care to experience again, but I am grateful I did. The experience, particularly what I carried from its conclusion, was a storm. If Jesus had caused the waters of the storm to subside immediately following the ambush, there would have been nothing to learn—I would not have developed perseverance, and it would not have brought forth maturity in me.

In the storm, amidst the trials of our faith, we can be confident that we are developing perseverance.

Isn't this the great mystery of our faith? During the violence of the storm, we cry out for God, and sometimes, there isn't an immediate response that we expect. However, in time, the response arrives. And in revelation we understand that the storm was more important than what caused it because ultimately, the great lesson of seeking Him, waiting, and persevering is conforming us into the image of Jesus.

The great lesson of seeking Him, waiting, and persevering is conforming us into the image of Jesus.

Chapter 11

VICTORY!

"Yours, O LORD, is the greatness, The power and the glory, The victory and the majesty; For all that is in heaven and earth is Yours; Yours is the kingdom, O LORD, And You are exalted as head over all."

1 Chronicles 29:11 (*NKJV*)

On June 3, 2012, our commercial flight touched down at Colorado Springs Airport. The doors opened and the soldiers began walking down the ramp to freedom, delivered from a year of toil and hardship. I watched as I stood in the aisle and reflected on the last year of my life. The events of 14 July 2011 briefly entered my mind, however, as I witnessed my last soldier exiting the plane, the thought exited just as quickly. Every single one of my men that boarded the outbound flight a year earlier had returned and was exiting now.

A Year Later

Gone was the shame I had felt in the wake of that fateful operation in Sur that day, delivered by the promise that "there is now no condemnation for those who are in Christ Jesus" (Romans 8:1, *ESV*). In that moment, condemnation had been replaced with joy that I (largely a mule), had been used by the God of the Universe for His good and perfect purposes.

Just as the diligent farmer referred to in 2 Timothy, I had spent the final ten months of the deployment planting in the field God had allotted me. Following Sur, before each mission, I prayed. Each Thursday night, I hosted a Bible study with regular—in some cases, abundant—platoon participation.

As I took my first step off the plane, onto the same tarmac I had crossed when leaving a year earlier, Sur was stowed in the testimony of His story. I thought about one of my favorite verses from the Bible: "I waited patiently for the Lord; he turned to me and heard my cry. He lifted me out of the slimy pit, out of the mud and mire; he set my feet on a rock and gave me a firm place to stand. He put a new song in my mouth, a hymn of praise to our God" (Psalm 40:1-3).

You Can't Ignore Trouble

You can't ignore trouble. Let me say that again: You cannot ignore trouble. When you are in trouble, it is there, and it is not going anywhere. Trouble may look different in individual human lives, but the effect is the same. Stress, anxiety, fear, challenge, and even death, encompass trouble. Trouble has been consistent and indiscriminate since its conception in the Garden of Eden, at the fall of man. Trouble has molded humanity's greatest implosion as well as its greatest resolve. It is malignant, has no selection, and in our broken world, will continue to be woven into the genetic makeup of the human condition.

Jesus emphatically said: "In this world you will have trouble. But take heart! I have overcome the world" (John 16:33). If He who lives in us is greater, and has overcome this world, what can this world or our enemy hurl our way that we cannot defeat?

Stress, anxiety, fear, challenge, and even death, encompass trouble. Trouble has been consistent and indiscriminate since its conception in the Garden of Eden, at the fall of man.

Before I ever walked into Sur on 14 July 2011, the battle was already won. Abandon yourself to God and live in victory!

AFTERWORD

I thought about the word, "forward," shortly after we returned from the deployment. The word came to me as I thought about God going before us throughout our time in Afghanistan. You see, in the United States, where there is crime, we have police to fight it. Where there is a fire, we have firemen to fight it. When there is a war, we have soldiers to fight it. All of these who serve are forward of the people, responding to and handling their respective responsibilities. In thinking about this further, I realized that there is no one forward of them. They are literally on the front lines.

When I was growing up in Southern California, I distinctly remember an incident in North Hollywood in which two bank robbers emerged from the bank they had just robbed, and indiscriminately began firing at civilians. In that moment, the police were the last line of defense. They were quickly dispatched and endured a bloody slugfest with the violent robbers, having inserted themselves between them and the civilians. Several officers were fatally wounded in bringing the murderous violence and chaos to an end. The innocent civilians had been helpless against these two men. Had it not been for the police being forward of them, the robbers would have been able to inflict upon them whatever evil they ultimately desired.

A month after returning to Colorado Springs, a massive forest fire erupted in the mountains to the West that shadow our beautiful city. On one particular Tuesday, the winds were so high that the fire began jumping the fire lines. The fire was literally being carried through the air and spreading rapidly. An apocalyptic smoke rose to the sky, blotting out the sun on a biblical proportion. I remember watching C-130 cargo planes from nearby Peterson Air Force Base, carrying tons of fire retardant, flying into the massive plume of smoke consuming the sky. I couldn't believe how brave those pilots were, as they flew into darkness, with smoke obscuring their vision, in order to drop a little defense on the epic blaze. One by one, I would watch them disappear into the smoke only to emerge minutes later, their propellers whipping smoke up over the wings as they desperately climbed from the grim clutches of the blaze. The whole city was at a standstill, witnessing the heroism of the pilots. As we stood defenseless on the ground, these pilots were on the front lines—forward of us.

Similarly, in the wake of 9/11, our brave police officers and firefighters responded to, and in many cases, gave their lives as they ran in while everyone else was running out. It was also in the wake of 9/11, that our soldiers deployed to go on the offensive in Afghanistan against those who brought horror to our country on that infamous day. Our nation was at war, and our soldiers would be going forward of their countrymen to fight. Mothers and fathers could tuck their children in at night knowing that freedom would endure, because half a world away, soldiers were forward of them ensuring it would.

All of these things rushed to mind as I thought about the word, "forward." But I began to think, *if all of these individuals are forward of the defenseless, then God would certainly have to be forward of them.* You see, when you are forward, that is it. No one else is going to move beyond you to engage in the fight. You are the front line. It is at that point that you realize the only one beside you and in front of you is God.

As I thought about that, I reflected back on Sur. Physically, we were the ones forward. It was literally nighttime back in the United States as we walked into Sur. While my family and friends were sound asleep, I was forward of them on a combat patrol. But forward of me was the Lord.

In any and all the negative situations, hurt, or pain we encounter on Earth—the sudden and unexpected loss of a child or loved one, loss of a job, dissolving of a marriage, rebellious children—God is before us. In Psalm 23:4, David, a man living in habitual embattlement, conveyed this so clearly, saying, "Even though I walk through the valley of the shadow of death, I will fear no evil, for you are with me; your rod and your staff, they comfort me."

As I write this now, I am relying on the fact that God is before me. Recently, I resigned my commission as a United States Army officer, walking away from a promising career that promised promotion, advancement, and a lucrative retirement package in the future. I left to attend seminary and to one day, by God's grace, plant and establish a church. Though I felt led of God to do all this, more questions than answers came with this decision.

As a practical thinker, in facing this season of preparation, I have been consumed with anxiety and worry over having enough money for seminary and to live, in general. It has not been easy. But I know that I didn't walk into Sur alone on 14 July 2011, and I know that I am not walking into this alone either. God has never abandoned me.

God is always forward of you and I. He knows what we need. He knows our hearts. I know it is hard, but when we are in something that we do not understand, need something we can't seem to obtain, or just simply need a miracle, these are the times to lean on Him most. The thing that seems easiest to do is to just sit in it, consumed in depression about it, scrambling to make it happen on our own. But what is truly easier (and more importantly, brings the most peace), is getting on our knees before Him, presenting these matters to Him from a thankful, abandoned heart, and waiting patiently for Him. The Lord will not fail us because perfection knows nothing of failure.

CPSIA information can be obtained at www.ICGtesting.com
Printed in the USA
LVOW07s0616141016

508396LV00003B/3/P